DAILY PRAYER PROJECT

Animating a life of prayer through the manifold beauty of the church

The Daily Prayer Project's Living Prayer Periodicals feature daily morning and evening prayer guides for the week. These guides are used throughout the current season of the Christian year. Their simplicity, brevity, and repetition facilitate transformative patterns of prayer in everyday life.

IN THIS EDITION

Scan for complimentary digital edition

CO-DIRECTOR

Joel Littlepage

CO-DIRECTOR

Ashley Williams

EDITOR

Russ Whitfield

CURATOR & COPYEDITOR

Victoria Emily Jones

ARTANDTHEOLOGY.ORG

DESIGNER

Lauren Shea Little

ATLAS MINOR DESIGN STUDIO

The Daily Prayer Project is produced as a ministry of Grace Mosaic in Northeast Washington, DC. Grace Mosaic is a congregation of the Grace DC Network.

CREDITS

Advent

DECEMBER 1-24, 2024

Advent, from the Latin *adventus*, means "coming" or "visitation." As followers of Jesus Christ, we live in between two visitations: the first coming of the Son of God in Bethlehem and his long-awaited second coming. We are waiting for the "day of the Lord," when creation will be healed, the dead will be raised, and all of us together will be ushered into the life of the world to come. This waiting frames our experience in this preparatory, watchful, somber, and joyful season before the luminous celebrations of Christmas and Epiphany.

2024-25 CHRISTIAN YEAR

ADVENT

DEC 1-24

CHRISTMAS & EPIPHANY

DEC 25-MAR 4

LENT

MAR 5-APR 19

EASTER

APR 20-JUN 7

PENTECOST

JUN 8

ORDINARY TIME

JUN 9-NOV 29

Advent Moon

ANGIER BROCK

Let the coming of the One
who arranges Orion and the Pleiades
begin in darkness.
Let the night be cold, with drifts of snow.
Let there be one lily blooming,
and whispered messages, and kneeling.

The fierce earth spins in expectation
beneath the long night's moon, Advent moon.
Like the restless fox crossing frosted meadows,
the silvered owl in focused, silent flight,
each of us is hungry.
In rooms of untold longing,
we sing our seasoned carols,
watch, and wait.

Let the coming of the One
who kindles fires of hope,
whose faithfulness runs far beyond our sight,
be like the coming of a child.
Let there be milk, forgiveness, quiet arms.
Come quickly, Love, our dearest deep
and sweetest dawning.
Come, fill us with your light.

Commissioned in 2013 by Bruton Parish Church in Williamsburg,
Virginia, as a choral anthem, with music by Cecilia McDowall

Advent Lectionary

SUN	FIRST SUNDAY OF ADVENT	Dec 1	Ps. 25:1–10	Jer. 33:14–16	Luke 21:25–36; 1 Thess. 3:9–13
MON	CREATION & NEW CREATION	Dec 2	Ps. 1	Gen. 1:1–26	Rev. 21:1–5
TUE	IMAGE OF GOD	Dec 3	Ps. 2	Gen. 1:27–2:3	Heb. 1:1–4
WED	THE CURSE	Dec 4	Ps. 3	Gen. 3:1–21	John 10:7–18
THU	THE PEACE	Dec 5	Ps. 4	Gen. 4:1–16	Heb. 12:22–29
FRI	THE FLOOD	Dec 6	Ps. 5	Gen. 7:1–10, 17–24	Luke 17:22–37
SAT	THE SON OF ABRAHAM	Dec 7	Ps. 6	Gen. 11:27–12:9	Gal. 3:8–14
SUN	SECOND SUNDAY OF ADVENT	Dec 8	Luke 1:68–79	Mal. 3:1–4	Luke 3:1–6; Phil. 1:3–11
MON	THE LION OF JUDAH	Dec 9	Ps. 7	Gen. 49:1, 8–12	Rev. 5:1–10
TUE	THE EXODUS	Dec 10	Ps. 8	Exod. 1:1–14; 2:23–25	Luke 4:16–21
WED	THE DIVINE WARRIOR	Dec 11	Ps. 9	Exod. 14:10–14	John 16:28–33
THU	THE TABERNACLE	Dec 12	Ps. 10	Exod. 40:33–38	Rev. 21:22–22:5
FRI	THE PRIEST	Dec 13	Ps. 11	Exod. 28:1–5	Heb. 9:11–14
SAT	THE SACRIFICE	Dec 14	Ps. 12	Lev. 16:29–34	Heb. 9:23–28

Advent Lectionary

SUN	GAUDETE SUNDAY (THIRD SUNDAY OF ADVENT)	Dec 15	Isa. 12:2–6	Zeph. 3:14–20	Luke 3:7–18; Phil. 4:4–7
MON	THE PROPHET	Dec 16	Ps. 13	Deut. 18:9–15	John 6:60–69
TUE	THE SON OF DAVID	Dec 17	Ps. 14	2 Sam. 7:1–13	Rev. 22:12–20
WED	THE SERVANT OF THE LORD	Dec 18	Ps. 15	Isa. 42:1–9	Luke 7:18–23
THU	THE PURIFIER	Dec 19	Ps. 16	Mal. 4:1–6	Luke 1:1–25
FRI	THE PROMISED OFFSPRING	Dec 20	Ps. 17	2 Kings 17:18–23; 25:8–11	Matt. 1:1–23
SAT	THE HEALER	Dec 21	Ps. 18	Isa. 62:6–12	Luke 1:26–45
SUN	FOURTH SUNDAY OF ADVENT	Dec 22	Ps. 80:1–7	Mic. 5:2–5a	Luke 1:39–55; Heb. 10:5–10
MON	THE SAVIOR	Dec 23	Ps. 19	Isa. 62:6–12	Luke 1:26–45
TUE	CHRISTMAS EVE	Dec 24	Ps. 96	Isa. 9:2–7	Titus 2:11–14; Luke 2:1–20

A Season for Those Who Long

BY JOEL LITTLEPAGE

"Watch therefore, for you know neither the day nor the hour."—Matthew 25:13

A twig snaps in the forest and the doe's neck whips around. A teacher's voice trails off and the sudden silence makes the distracted students look up with startled awareness. The whistle at the crosswalk sends a spark to the heart and the driver's foot to the brakes. The snap, the silence, the whistle—they all call back to attention.

"Watch," says Jesus. Keep alert, stay vigilant, don't fall asleep, don't be lulled by the status quo of the world and its song of utopic pleasure. This world is not a utopia; despite all its beauty, it is a bleeding world awaiting the suture, a crying world awaiting a tender hush, a clamoring world awaiting a peaceful silence.

When you spend time listening to the words of Jesus from the pages of the Gospels, you might be struck by his apocalyptic imagination and fervor. The verse above comes from our Lord's quintessential Advent parable, traditionally called the Parable of the Ten Virgins (Matt. 25:1–13). In the story, ten women are called to wait for the arrival of the bridegroom so that they may join in the wedding banquet. Half of them neglect to bring extra oil for the long wait, whereas the other half stay prepared and ready. When the bridegroom suddenly comes back in the middle of the night, the five prepared women enter into the feast while the five unprepared are left outside, excluded due to their running around and scrambling to get ready.

The snap of this story is echoed throughout Jesus's parables and well into the later New Testament letters as well: "While people are saying, 'There is peace and security,' then sudden destruction will come upon them as labor pains come upon a pregnant woman. . . . So then let us not sleep, as others do, but let us keep awake and be sober. For those who sleep, sleep at night, and those who get drunk, are drunk at night. But since we belong to the day, let us be sober" (1 Thess. 5:3a, 6–8a). When we do not pay attention to our lives and to questions of ultimacy, it is quite possible for us to live completely "without," carried about by the allure of our biggest fans' effusive opinions, drunk with affluence, and shackled to the modern technological engine. But if we receive the mercy of the divine shout (or silence), if we heed the call to pay attention to our lives and the "signs of the times," then other possibilities emerge.

Those other possibilities always flow from a posture of humility. Many (most?) of us are too wrapped up in our doings to pay attention to God's. We are so often enamored by our own little fiefdoms that we are not aware of the bigger reality of the kingdom of God. We are more interested in maintaining a facade of health and prosperity while ignoring the cancerous realities that waste away our cities, homes, and congregations: poverty, neglect, abuse, pride, hoarding, dishonesty, alienation, and hunger. Jesus invites—no, commands—us to name each and every one of these realities and to live for a bigger vision of life than we could ever possibly embody with our own resources. To admit that we are in need of deeper transformation and help.

Advent is the season for those who need help. For those who long for homeliness in a world so often marked by abandonment. For those who come to realize—year after year, again and again—that the patterns of their lives need realignment to the upside-down kingdom that Jesus proclaimed, a kingdom that is not of this world and that refuses to make peace with its evil and forgetful ways.

Advent is the season for those who need hope. For those who realize that naming everything wrong will not crush us but will instead liberate us to receive the promise of God's love where it counts: in real life. For those who long to see justice roll down like mighty rivers (Amos 5:24), for those who long to see guns melted into shovels (Isa. 2:4), for those who long to see the one called Faithful and True riding on his white horse to bring war against everything that needs to be banished from the Creator's world (Rev. 19:11).

Advent is the season for those who want the future now. For those who have received the *arrabon* (Greek for "downpayment," Eph. 1:14) of the Spirit, who urges us to walk into the world of the future in the mundanity and madness of the present. For those who are paying attention to the next step where God is leading by remaining alert to what God is up to, attentive to God's voice. For those who are so captivated by the possibilities of "shall be" that they can't help but keep their lamps trimmed and burning, waiting for the crack of the door and the arrival of the Healer.

In this Advent edition we practice Jesus's command to "watch and pray." We've made some changes to our design and slight modifications to our format in an effort to provide more spaciousness to the layout and make things easier to see. I want to thank our staff designer, Lauren Shea Little, for her continued artistry and attentive care for all of us who pray together.

Stanley Fung's *Look forward to the coming of God* (gracing the cover of this edition and highlighted in the Gallery) provides a fitting doorway into the attentive waiting of this season. We are led into prayer by Kari Kristina Reeves, who cries out, "Grant us more of your Spirit as we wait upon your second coming. Give us anticipation and hope for the day when you will right all wrongs." In the Practices, Gregory Thompson's "Nurturing the Hidden Life" invites us to practice contemplation in the everyday of our lives. Finally, in the Songbook, "Come Light Our Hearts" is a simple and beautiful prayer for those waiting for the Light of the World. May all these resources and more help us to more deeply "watch and pray." ⊃

JOEL LITTLEPAGE is the associate pastor of Grace Mosaic, laboring in the areas of worship and spiritual formation. A professional musician, he lives in the beautiful Fifth Ward of Washington, DC, with his wife, three sons, and a flock of chickens.

Prayers, Part 1

SUNDAY MORNING *to* WEDNESDAY EVENING

KERALA, INDIA

Ashish AB

Sunday Morning

LECTIONARY

DEC 1

FIRST SUNDAY OF

ADVENT

Ps. 25:1–10

Jer. 33:14–16

Luke 21:25–36;

1 Thess. 3:9–13

DEC 8

SECOND SUNDAY OF

ADVENT

Luke 1:46–55

Mal. 3:1–4

Luke 3:1–6;

Phil. 1:3–11

MORNING PRAYER

CALL

Lift up your heads, O gates!
And be lifted up, O ancient doors,
that the King of glory may come in.

Psalm 24:7

PSALM

Read the Psalm of the day.

THE O ANTIPHONS

O Emmanuel,
our King and our Lawgiver,
the hope of the nations and their Savior:
come and save us, O Lord our God.

Stanza from the O Antiphons (ca. 700), taken from The New Ancient Collects

ADORATION

SILENCE OR SONG

Seasonal song selections can be found on pp. 57-63.

LESSON

Read the New Testament passage of the day.

PRAYER

Heavenly Father,
Lord in heaven,
Spirit who dwells within:
this morning we worship you
as the Alpha and the Omega,
the Beginning and the End,
the First and the Last.
As our God who hears our prayers,
as our Master who attends to our cries,
as the Holy Spirit who groans within us,
we call upon you now.
Lord, in your mercy, hear our prayers.
Grant us more of your Spirit as we wait
upon your second coming.
Give us anticipation and hope for the day
when you will right all wrongs.

Teach us how to walk by faith and not by sight, and
help us to love our neighbors as we love ourselves.
Lord, fill us afresh with your Holy
Indwelling as we pray to you, the Alpha and the Omega:
Lord, in your mercy, hear our prayers.

A prayer of Kari Kristina Reeves, taken from *Canyon Road*

ABIDING

LECTIO DIVINA, VISIO DIVINA, OR PRAXIO DIVINA

Pause at the start of a new day. Enjoy communion with the living God:
Father, Son, and Holy Spirit. Listen for the voice of God in the scriptures.
Read. Meditate. Pray. Contemplate. Seek God's face.

PROMPTED PRAYER

- For openness to the way God
  wants to move in your life
- For joy and wonder at the beauty of the Incarnation
- For hesitant hearts to be drawn in by
  the gentle and lowly heart of Christ

THE LORD'S PRAYER

Our Father who art in heaven, hallowed be thy name.
Thy kingdom come, thy will be done,
on earth as it is in heaven.
Give us this day our daily bread;
and forgive us our debts, as we forgive our debtors.
And lead us not into temptation, but deliver us from evil.
For thine is the kingdom and the power
and the glory, forever. Amen.

BENEDICTION

He who testifies to these things says, "Surely I
am coming soon." Amen. Come, Lord Jesus! May
the grace of the Lord Jesus be with all. Amen.

Adapted from Revelation 22:20–21

LECTIONARY

DEC 15

GAUDETE SUNDAY
(THIRD SUNDAY OF
ADVENT)

Isa. 12:2–6

Zeph. 3:14–20

Luke 3:7–18;

Phil. 4:4–7

DEC 22

FOURTH SUNDAY OF
ADVENT

Ps. 80:1–7

Mic. 5:2–5a

Luke 1:39–55;

Heb. 10:5–10

MORNING PRAYER

Sunday Evening

LECTIONARY

DEC 1

FIRST SUNDAY OF

ADVENT

Ps. 25:1–10

Jer. 33:14–16

Luke 21:25–36;

1 Thess. 3:9–13

DEC 8

SECOND SUNDAY OF

ADVENT

Luke 1:46–55

Mal. 3:1–4

Luke 3:1–6;

Phil. 1:3–11

CALL

By day the LORD commands his steadfast love,
and at night his song is with me,
a prayer to the God of my life.

Psalm 42:8

PSALM

Read the Psalm of the day.

THE O ANTIPHONS

O Emmanuel,
our King and our Lawgiver,
the hope of the nations and their Savior:
come and save us, O Lord our God.

Taken from *The New Ancient Collects*

ADORATION

SILENCE OR SONG

Seasonal song selections can be found on pp. 57-63.

LESSON

Read the Old Testament passage of the day.

PRAYER

O God our deliverer,
you cast down the mighty,
and lift up those of no account:
as Elizabeth and Mary embraced
with songs of liberation,
so may we also be pregnant with your Spirit,
and affirm one another in hope for the world,
through Jesus Christ, Amen.

A prayer of Janet Morley of England, from *All Desires Known*

ABIDING

LECTIO DIVINA, VISIO DIVINA, OR PRAXIO DIVINA

Pause at the start of a new day. Enjoy communion with the living God: Father, Son, and Holy Spirit. Listen for the voice of God in the scriptures. Read. Meditate. Pray. Contemplate. Seek God's face.

INTERCESSORY PRAYER

Pray for the known needs of your church, neighborhood, city, and world.

BENEDICTION

May the God of hope fill you with all joy and peace in believing, so that by the power of the Holy Spirit you may abound in hope.

Romans 15:13

LECTIONARY

DEC 15

GAUDETE SUNDAY

(THIRD SUNDAY OF

ADVENT)

Isa. 12:2–6

Zeph. 3:14–20

Luke 3:7–18;

Phil. 4:4–7

DEC 22

FOURTH SUNDAY OF

ADVENT

Ps. 80:1–7

Mic. 5:2–5a

Luke 1:39–55;

Heb. 10:5–10

EVENING PRAYER

Monday Morning

LECTIONARY

DEC 2

CREATION & NEW
CREATION

Ps. 1

Gen. 1:1–26

Rev. 21:1–5

DEC 9

THE LION OF JUDAH

Ps. 7

Gen. 49:1, 8–12

Rev. 5:1–10

MORNING PRAYER

CALL

A voice cries: "In the wilderness
prepare the way of the LORD;
make straight in the desert a highway for our God."

Isaiah 40:3

PSALM

Read the Psalm of the day.

THE O ANTIPHONS

O Morning Star,
splendor of light eternal
and Sun of righteousness:
come and enlighten those who dwell in darkness
and the shadow of death.

Taken from *The New Ancient Collects*

ADORATION

SILENCE OR SONG

Seasonal song selections can be found on pp. 57–63.

LESSON

Read the Old Testament passage of the day.

PRAYER

When I'm down and helpless
When lies are reigning
When fear and indifference are growing
May your kingdom come!

When joy is missing
When love is missing
And unbelief is growing
May your kingdom come!

To the sick and lonely
To the imprisoned and tortured
May your kingdom come!

Into the churches
Into our praying, into our singing
May your kingdom come!

Into our hearts
Into our hands, into our eyes
May your kingdom come! Soon!

A Czech Litany, taken from *Soul Weavings*

ABIDING

LECTIO DIVINA, VISIO DIVINA, OR PRAXIO DIVINA

Pause at the start of a new day. Enjoy communion with the living God:
Father, Son, and Holy Spirit. Listen for the voice of God in the scriptures.
Read. Meditate. Pray. Contemplate. Seek God's face.

PROMPTED PRAYER

- For eyes to see and tend to "the least of these"
- For the safety of travelers during the holiday season
- For protection against despair and hopelessness in a world that is often sad and confusing

THE LORD'S PRAYER

Our Father who art in heaven, hallowed be thy name.
Thy kingdom come, thy will be done,
on earth as it is in heaven.
Give us this day our daily bread;
and forgive us our debts, as we forgive our debtors.
And lead us not into temptation, but deliver us from evil.
For thine is the kingdom and the power
and the glory, forever. Amen.

BENEDICTION

Salvation is nearer to us now than when we first
believed. The night is far gone; the day is at hand.
So then let us cast off the works of darkness
and put on the armor of light. May you go from
this place walking in the light of the Lord.

Adapted from Romans 13:11–12

LECTIONARY

DEC 16

THE PROPHET

Ps. 13

Deut. 18:9–15

John 6:60–69

DEC 23

THE SAVIOR

Ps. 19

Isa. 62:6–12

Luke 1:26–45

MORNING PRAYER

Monday Evening

EVENING PRAYER

CALL

I remember your name in the night, O LORD,
and keep your law.

Psalm 119:55

PSALM

Read the Psalm of the day.

THE O ANTIPHONS

O Morning Star,
splendor of light eternal
and Sun of righteousness:
come and enlighten those who dwell in darkness
and the shadow of death.

Taken from *The New Ancient Collects*

ADORATION

SILENCE OR SONG

Seasonal song selections can be found on pp. 57–63.

LESSON

Read the New Testament passage of the day.

PRAYER

CONFESSION: Holy and loving God,
we have dwelt in darkness
and preferred it to the light;
we have been proud of our accomplishments
and despaired over our shortcomings.
Smooth down the mountains of our pride,
and lift up the valleys of our doubts.
Open a path in the wilderness of our lives
that we might find our way to you again.
Refine us and prepare us once again
for life in your kingdom.
Hear our prayer, O Lord. Amen.

Source unknown

ASSURANCE: Comfort, comfort my people, says your God. Speak tenderly to Jerusalem, and cry to her that her warfare is ended, that her iniquity is pardoned, that she has received from the LORD's hand double for all her sins. A voice cries: "In the wilderness prepare the way of the LORD; make straight in the desert a highway for our God. Every valley shall be lifted up, and every mountain and hill be made low; the uneven ground shall become level, and the rough places a plain. And the glory of the LORD shall be revealed, and all flesh shall see it together, for the mouth of the LORD has spoken."

Isaiah 40:1-5

ABIDING

LECTIO DIVINA, VISIO DIVINA, OR PRAXIO DIVINA

Pause at the start of a new day. Enjoy communion with the living God: Father, Son, and Holy Spirit. Listen for the voice of God in the scriptures. Read. Meditate. Pray. Contemplate. Seek God's face.

INTERCESSORY PRAYER

Pray for the known needs of your church, neighborhood, city, and world.

BENEDICTION

The ransomed of the LORD shall return and come to Zion with singing; everlasting joy shall be upon their heads; they shall obtain gladness and joy, and sorrow and sighing shall flee away. Rest now in the joy of the Lord.

Adapted from Isaiah 35:10

LECTIONARY

DEC 16

THE PROPHET

Ps. 13

Deut. 18:9–15

John 6:60–69

DEC 23

THE SAVIOR

Ps. 19

Isa. 62:6–12

Luke 1:26–45

EVENING PRAYER

Tuesday Morning

LECTIONARY

DEC 3

IMAGE OF GOD

Ps. 2

Gen. 1:27–2:3

Heb. 1:1–4

DEC 10

THE EXODUS

Ps. 8

Exod. 1:1–14; 2:23–25

Luke 4:16–21

CALL

I waited patiently for the LORD;
he inclined to me and heard my cry.

Psalm 40:1

PSALM

Read the Psalm of the day.

THE O ANTIPHONS

O Wisdom,
coming forth from the mouth of the Most High,
reaching from one end to the other,
mightily and sweetly ordering all things:
come and teach us the way of understanding.

Taken from *The New Ancient Collects*

ADORATION

SILENCE OR SONG

Seasonal song selections can be found on pp. 57–63.

LESSON

Read the New Testament passage of the day.

PRAYER

Oh Lord, you know just how I feel
Know just how I feel
Oh Lord, you said you'd answer prayer
Said you'd answer prayer
Oh Lord, I'm coming to you again
Coming to you again
Oh Lord, we sure do need you now
Sure do need you now

Adapted from a prayer sung by Fannie Lou Hamer (1917–1977) of Ruleville, Mississippi, taken from *Songs My Mother Taught Me.* Click here or scan the QR code to the left to hear a recording of Ms. Hamer singing this prayer.

ABIDING

LECTIO DIVINA, VISIO DIVINA, OR PRAXIO DIVINA

Pause at the start of a new day. Enjoy communion with the living God: Father, Son, and Holy Spirit. Listen for the voice of God in the scriptures. Read. Meditate. Pray. Contemplate. Seek God's face.

PROMPTED PRAYER
- For parents to experience joy in the nurture of their children
- For schoolteachers, administrators, staff, and students
- For deeper understanding of our relationship to the environment and kinship with creation

THE LORD'S PRAYER

Our Father who art in heaven, hallowed be thy name.
Thy kingdom come, thy will be done,
on earth as it is in heaven.
Give us this day our daily bread;
and forgive us our debts, as we forgive our debtors.
And lead us not into temptation, but deliver us from evil.
For thine is the kingdom and the power
and the glory, forever. Amen.

BENEDICTION

Strengthen the weak hands, and make firm the feeble knees. Say to those who have an anxious heart, "Be strong; fear not! Behold, your God will come with vengeance, with the recompense of God. He will come and save you." May your whole body and spirit be strengthened in the power of God as you go through the rest of your day.

Adapted from Isaiah 35:3–4

LECTIONARY

DEC 17

THE SON OF DAVID

Ps. 14

2 Sam. 7:1–13

Rev. 22:12–20

DEC 24

CHRISTMAS EVE

Ps. 96

Isa. 9:2–7

Titus 2:11–14;

Luke 2:1–20

MORNING PRAYER

Tuesday Evening

LECTIONARY

DEC 3

IMAGE OF GOD

Ps. 2

Gen. 1:27–2:3

Heb. 1:1–4

DEC 10

THE EXODUS

Ps. 8

Exod. 1:1–14; 2:23–25

Luke 4:16–21

CALL

Come, bless the LORD, all you servants of the LORD,
who stand by night in the house of the LORD!
Psalm 134:1

PSALM

Read the Psalm of the day.

THE O ANTIPHONS

O Wisdom,
coming forth from the mouth of the Most High,
reaching from one end to the other,
mightily and sweetly ordering all things:
come and teach us the way of understanding.

Taken from *The New Ancient Collects*

ADORATION

SILENCE OR SONG

Seasonal song selections can be found on pp. 57–63.

LESSON

Read the Old Testament passage of the day.

PRAYER

Lord, my God, Light of the blind and Strength of the weak; indeed, also, Light of those who see, and Strength of the strong: listen to my soul, and hear it crying out of the depths. Lord, help us to turn and seek you, for you have not forsaken your creatures the way we have forsaken you, our Creator. Let us turn and seek you, for we know you are here in our hearts, when we confess to you, when we cast ourselves on you, and weep at your feet, after all our rugged ways. And you gently wipe away our tears, and we weep the more for joy, because you, Lord, who made us, remake and comfort us. Lord, hear my prayer, and grant that I may most entirely love you, and rescue me, Lord, from every temptation, even to the end. Amen.

A prayer of Augustine (354–430) of Hippo (present-day Algeria),
taken from *Prayers through the Centuries*

ABIDING

LECTIO DIVINA, VISIO DIVINA, OR PRAXIO DIVINA

Pause at the start of a new day. Enjoy communion with the living God:
Father, Son, and Holy Spirit. Listen for the voice of God in the scriptures.
Read. Meditate. Pray. Contemplate. Seek God's face.

INTERCESSORY PRAYER

Pray for the known needs of your church, neighborhood, city, and world.

BENEDICTION

Wait for the LORD; be strong, and let your heart
take courage; wait for the LORD! May you rest
now in the sure promise of his return.

Adapted from Psalm 27:14

LECTIONARY

DEC 17

THE SON OF DAVID

Ps. 14

2 Sam. 7:1–13

Rev. 22:12–20

DEC 24

CHRISTMAS EVE

Ps. 96

Isa. 9:2–7

Titus 2:11–14;

Luke 2:1–20

EVENING PRAYER

Wednesday Morning

MORNING PRAYER

CALL

"My soul magnifies the Lord,
and my spirit rejoices in God my Savior!"
Luke 1:46–47

PSALM

Read the Psalm of the day.

THE O ANTIPHONS

O Key of David
and Scepter of the house of Israel,
what you open no one can shut;
what you shut no one can open.
***Come and lead the prisoners from the prison house,
who dwell in darkness and the shadow of death.***
Taken from *The New Ancient Collects*

ADORATION

SILENCE OR SONG

Seasonal song selections can be found on pp. 57–63.

LESSON

Read the Old Testament passage of the day.

PRAYER

CONFESSION: Father, for those sins I have committed against you, consciously or unconsciously, in practicing evil, in cooperation with works of darkness, or in any other way that is displeasing to you and not aligned with your heavenly kingdom, please forgive me, and please grant me the liberty of your Holy Spirit at work in this area of my life.
A prayer of Kari Kristina Reeves, taken from *Canyon Road*

ASSURANCE: So Christ, having been offered once to bear the sins of many, will appear a second time, not to deal with sin but to save those who are eagerly waiting for him.
Hebrews 9:28

ABIDING

LECTIO DIVINA, VISIO DIVINA, OR PRAXIO DIVINA

Pause at the start of a new day. Enjoy communion with the living God: Father, Son, and Holy Spirit. Listen for the voice of God in the scriptures. Read. Meditate. Pray. Contemplate. Seek God's face.

PROMPTED PRAYER

- For unmarried people in your church community
- For the flourishing of marriages and families in your neighborhood
- For those without a strong support system and the opportunity to move toward them in love

THE LORD'S PRAYER

Our Father who art in heaven, hallowed be thy name.
Thy kingdom come, thy will be done,
on earth as it is in heaven.
Give us this day our daily bread;
and forgive us our debts, as we forgive our debtors.
And lead us not into temptation, but deliver us from evil.
For thine is the kingdom and the power
and the glory, forever. Amen.

BENEDICTION

"Listen to me, O house of Jacob, all the remnant of the house of Israel, who have been borne by me from before your birth, carried from the womb; even to your old age I am he, and to gray hairs I will carry you. I have made, and I will bear; I will carry and will save." May you go forward today as one carried by your Maker.

Adapted from Isaiah 46:3-4

LECTIONARY

DEC 18

THE SERVANT OF THE LORD

Ps. 15
Isa. 42:1–9
Luke 7:18–23

MORNING PRAYER

Wednesday Evening

LECTIONARY

DEC 4

THE CURSE

Ps. 3

Gen. 3:1–21

John 10:7–18

DEC 11

THE DIVINE WARRIOR

Ps. 9

Exod. 14:10–14

John 16:28–33

CALL

It is good to give thanks to the LORD,
to sing praises to your name, O Most High;
to declare your steadfast love in the morning,
and your faithfulness by night.

Psalm 92:1–2

PSALM

Read the Psalm of the day.

THE O ANTIPHONS

O Key of David
and Scepter of the house of Israel,
what you open no one can shut;
what you shut no one can open.
Come and lead the prisoners from the prison house,
who dwell in darkness and the shadow of death.

Taken from *The New Ancient Collects*

ADORATION

SILENCE OR SONG

Seasonal song selections can be found on pp. 57–63.

LESSON

Read the New Testament passage of the day.

PRAYER

O God, in your love, you have kept me vigorously and
joyfully at work in the day now done,
and now you send me joyful and contented
into silence and inactivity;
grant me to find happiness in you in all
my solitary and quiet hours.
In your strength, O God, I bid farewell to all.
The past you know; I leave it at your feet.
Grant me grace to respond to your divine call; to leave
all that is dear on earth and go out alone to you.
"Behold, I come quickly," says the Lord.
Amen. Come, Lord Jesus.

A prayer of Rev. Premananda Ananth Nath Sen (1876–?) of Calcutta,

India, adapted from *Morning, Noon and Night*. Rev. Sen was a Hindu convert to Christianity who became a pastor and established a hospital for those who suffered from leprosy that still survives today. This particular prayer was offered toward the end of his life.

ABIDING

LECTIO DIVINA, VISIO DIVINA, OR PRAXIO DIVINA

Pause at the start of a new day. Enjoy communion with the living God: Father, Son, and Holy Spirit. Listen for the voice of God in the scriptures. Read. Meditate. Pray. Contemplate. Seek God's face.

PRAYER OF MINDFULNESS

Throughout the history of the church, Christians have incorporated practices of prayer that call to mind God's presence in the moment, humbly and gratefully review the time that has passed, and look forward to the gift of another day. Pray through these prompts slowly, giving time to each step of the practice.

1. Become aware of God's presence.
2. Review the day with gratitude.
3. Pay attention to your emotions.
4. Choose one feature of the day and pray from it.
5. Look toward tomorrow.

BENEDICTION

The LORD bless you and keep you;
the LORD make his face to shine upon you
and be gracious to you;
the LORD lift up his countenance upon you
and give you peace.

Numbers 6:24–26

LECTIONARY

DEC 18

THE SERVANT OF THE
LORD
Ps. 15
Isa. 42:1–9
Luke 7:18–23

EVENING PRAYER

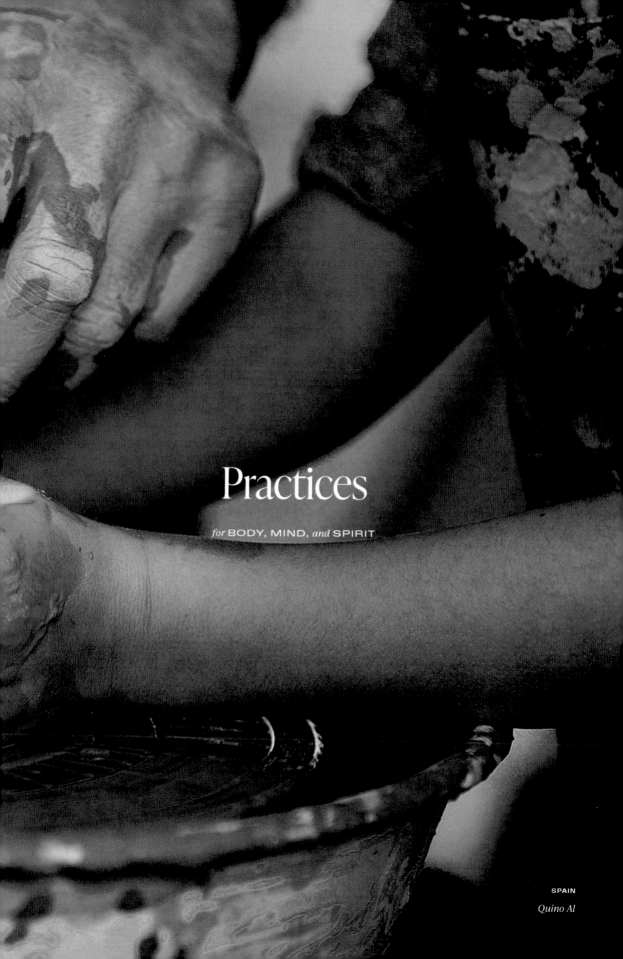

Practices

for BODY, MIND, *and* SPIRIT

SPAIN

Quino Al

A Friend in Waiting

BY ASHLEY WILLIAMS

MEDITATION

It is a peculiar scene: Two women with two extraordinary pregnancies. One is a teenager whose womb is like the world at creation: teeming with life formed by fiat. The other is a woman "advanced in years," withered by the reproach of barrenness, and now her frown is turned upright with every backflip of the infant growing inside her belly. Pregnancy is one of the most remarkable windows into the discipline of waiting. Juxtaposed with the deafening silence of a waiting Israel longing for her Messiah, a pregnant Elizabeth greets her cousin Mary with this exclamatory benediction: "Blessed are you among women and blessed is the fruit of your womb! . . . And blessed is she who believed that there would be a fulfillment of what was spoken to her from the Lord" (Luke 1:42b, 45).

With their extended midsections awaiting the arrival of sons, these women are companions to those of us who wait. Some of us are waiting for pregnancies. Others are waiting for marriages, jobs, good news, etc. What do we need in the vulnerable labor of waiting? We see it clearly in this text: encouragement in community. We need friends who know intimately what we are waiting for and who speak the same benediction over us: "Blessed are you who believed . . ." Paul asks the Galatian Christians to "carry each other's burdens" (Gal. 6:2). James says that healing is in the praying of one another (James 5:16). The writer of Hebrews also confirms that encouragement in a community helps "spur one another on" (Heb. 10:24–25).

In the season of Advent, we are looking toward the fulfillment of God's promises. We are hoping and waiting for the redemption of mind, body, and soul. Waiting, by nature, is complex. To continue in hope, we need the community of faith and her benedictions to help us along the way.

EXPLORATION

How can we foster habits of encouragement in our friendships? Consider these questions and suggested practices to embody this Advent season:

1. Use scriptures to encourage others. Being generally more fluent in criticism and complaint, many of us lack proficiency in

Mary and Elizabeth are companions to those of us who wait.

the language of encouragement. What should we do? Paul tells us that "through endurance and through the encouragement of the Scriptures we might have hope" (Rom. 15:4). Try memorizing passages of scripture that have encouraged you in the silence and darkness of waiting and speak those words to others. Just as God's word brings life in the void of worlds and wombs, so too does his word bring life to the weary.

2. Practice presence in friendships so your encouragement can be specific and personal. Spend time thinking about those around you and where you see the Lord's handiwork in their lives. Take notes, send texts, write cards. When you see goodness and godliness in others, tell them! It is proper and necessary in our communities to lovingly point out areas of sin and opportunities for change, but it is equally vital to admonish and affirm where we see growth in spiritual maturity and greater alignment with the image of Christ.

3. Do not grow weary in encouraging others. Unfortunately, we live in a society that often functions with a scarcity mindset—if there is encouragement for one, there is not enough encouragement for another. But that is not so in the economy of God's kingdom. When we bless others, we embody the joy of giving that God desires to cultivate within us. The discipline of blessing others forms us to believe that just as God loves a cheerful giver and honors the generosity of his people, he loves a cheerful encourager and blesses those who bless others.

When we encourage one another, we are participating in the work of the Spirit, comforting others toward hope amid silence and waiting (Phil. 2:1). May our words be sprinkled with benedictions for those awaiting, with wearied hope, the sure appearance of our promised Messiah. ⊃

ASHLEY WILLIAMS is the co-director of the Daily Prayer Project and a ministry coordinator for Grace Mosaic, a multiethnic church in Washington, DC. She is also a practicing spiritual director, certified through Leadership Transformations Inc.

Nurturing the Hidden Life

BY DR. GREGORY THOMPSON

MEDITATION

The season of Advent can, for many of us, have a contradictory feel to it. On one hand, we are told that it is a season of waiting; a season of contemplative silence and penitential stillness in anticipation of the Christmas celebration that is to come. And we try. We light Advent candles. We play Advent music. We pray Advent prayers. And we try, oh how we try, to settle ourselves into an Advent frame of heart. On the other hand, we know from experience that it is one of the most frantic and exhausting seasons of the year; a season of distracting noise and endless motion in preparation for the Christmas celebration that is to come. We help children with school. We buy presents. We decorate rooms. We send cards. We finish year-end work projects. And we fall into bed, desperate to settle into a few hours of forgetful sleep. In my own life, both of these are true. And not only true, but necessary; each is given to me by God. As a result, I have spent the better part of every Advent of my adult life with the frustrating sense of being pulled apart—pulled inward into silence even as I am pulled outward into a life of noise. And so every year a question arises within me: How can I learn to live both lives at once? How can I live in stillness and in motion at the same time?

In thinking of this, I turn, as I do every year, to Mary. Apart from our Lord, she is my absolute favorite person in the Bible. The first to welcome Christ. Faithful in nurturing his life within her. Confused and brokenhearted, and yet present with him from beginning to end. She is the first and perhaps loveliest of Jesus's followers. What we see most of her, however, takes place in that mysterious and holy time between the Annunciation (when she first learns of the hidden life growing within her) and the Nativity. And it is in this space—the space of Mary's own personal Advent—where we can learn about how to live our own Advent.

In one sense, Mary's life is, by any measure, out of control. Consider: She is a young woman, betrothed to a man, and yet pregnant (it seems) by another man. She takes refuge for several months in her relative Elizabeth's house, who, as you may remember, is navigating her own unexpected pregnancy and the crisis of a newly mute husband. Mary then

It is possible to live our ordinary, harried, and burdened lives and to experience the hidden life of Christ . . . precisely *there*.

has to travel while "great with child" to the distant city of Bethlehem with her husband and is unable to find a place to stay. During the stay, while lodging in a stable, she gives birth to her child, attended only by her husband. Shortly thereafter she finds herself playing host to a group of local shepherds and foreign princes who drop in for an impromptu baby shower. Oh, and don't forget that after the shower is over, an angel warns her husband that a murderous king is after them, and tells them to flee to Egypt. She, in other words, understands what it means to have a stressful Advent.

And yet *during all this*, Mary quietly nurtures the life of Christ within her. She dreams of motherhood. She lies in bed and watches her tummy grow. She puts Elizabeth's hand on her womb to feel the baby move. She adjusts her posture on the way to Bethlehem to give the baby room. She steps into the stable and begins to rearrange the place in anticipation. She looks at Joseph and says, "It's time." She makes room for her visitors. She prepares for the flight to Egypt. And each of these acts of attending to the presence of Christ takes place not apart from but *within* the burdens of her life.

I love this for two reasons. First, because it reminds us that our experience of Advent–the frustrating and embarrassing experience of struggling between contemplation and action–is actually original to Advent, fundamental to its very meaning; that this struggle, this longing, this weight is its essence. And as I enter into that struggle, seeking to hold the life of Christ in me together with my life in the world, I am actually doing Advent's essential work. And second, I love Mary's story because it reminds me that this work of Advent is within our reach. It is possible to live our ordinary, harried, and burdened lives and to experience the hidden life of Christ not elsewhere, but precisely *there*. And this means it is amid our lives–doing our jobs, tending our children, caring for our bodies, welcoming our neighbors, remembering our loved ones–and not in some idealized contemplative space, that Christ is present with us. It is here that the angel of the Lord says to us, as he said to Mary, "The Lord is with you." It is here that the mystery of Christ grows. It is here that God sends blessed guests, and necessary help. It is here that we will see the very face of Christ. ⊃

As we enter into this Advent life together, let's do so remembering that the Lord is with us, pondering and treasuring this presence and rejoicing in the secret knowledge that the hidden work we do now will, in time, bear the holiest of fruit. Consider a few of these practices to help nurture a hidden life with the Lord:

1. Dedicate some task you are doing to the Lord. Talk to him about the task before you begin and again when you are done. Do you become more aware of God in the process? How?

2. Practice the presence in interruptions. The intention to live in the presence of Christ is a way of saying, "I am here." Throughout the day, perhaps every time you are interrupted, tell God, "I am here." Remind yourself that you are in the presence of Jesus who had time for people who questioned and interrupted. Remember that some of Jesus's most gracious miracles occurred when he was interrupted. What is it like for you to offer yourself to be present to God during interruptions?

3. Decide to stop several times throughout your day to pay attention to God and practice his presence. Set a clock to remind you. Spend five minutes reading scripture, praying, or just being with Jesus. What is this like for you?

4. Develop some prayers that help you stay awake to God. For instance, find a verse or prayer that is your waking prayer, your in-the-shower prayer, your dressing prayer, your cooking prayer, your driving prayer, and so on. Let these prayers lead you into deeper encounters with the God who is there.

* Exploration suggestions are by Adele Ahlberg Calhoun and are excerpted from her *Spiritual Disciplines Handbook: Practices That Transform Us* (2015). Used with permission of IVP Formatio, conveyed through Copyright Clearance Center, Inc.

GREGORY THOMPSON (PhD, University of Virginia) is a pastor, scholar, artist, and producer whose work focuses on race and equity in the United States. He is the co-creator of *Union: The Musical*, a soul- and hip-hop-based musical about the 1968 Sanitation Workers' Strike, and the coauthor, with Duke L. Kwon, of *Reparations: A Christian Call for Repentance and Repair* (Brazos, 2021).

Gallery

for CONTEMPLATION

CHRISMON OIL LAMP

North Africa, 4th century

Terracotta, 1 5/16 × 4 3/16 × 2 9/16 in. (3.3 × 10.6 × 6.5 cm)

Walters Art Museum, Baltimore

Look forward to the coming of God (期待上帝)

BY STANLEY FUNG (馮君藍)

"Keep your lamps burning, . . . for the Son of Man is coming at an hour you do not expect." – LUKE 12:35, 40

CURATOR COMMENTARY

Stanley Fung (born 1961) is the pastor of Chinese Rhenish Church in Taipei, Taiwan, as well as an artist whose photography practice is part of his religious contemplation, he says. This photograph from his Dust Icons series shows a man holding a lit candle in the dark, staring forward with determination and expectation. He is waiting for the coming of Christ.

Watchfulness is a key theme in the New Testament—the call to be ready at all times for Christ's return; awake, alert, praying, standing fast in the faith, casting off evil works, persevering in what is good. Advent is a period in which Christians seek, with renewed focus, to cultivate a posture of readiness for this promised arrival.

Let us pray, in the words of the seventeenth-century English theologian Richard Baxter: "Keep us, O Lord, while we tarry on this earth, in a serious seeking after thee, and in an affectionate walking with thee, every day of our lives; that when thou comest, we may be found not hiding our talent, nor serving the flesh, nor yet asleep with our lamp unfurnished, but waiting and longing for our Lord, and glorious King, forever and ever."

LOOK FORWARD TO THE COMING OF GOD (期待上帝)
Stanley Fung (馮君藍)*, 2002*
Digital print on Hahnemühle fine art paper, 100 × 67.5 cm
www.stanleyfung-art.com

High Way

BY DONALD FURST

CURATOR COMMENTARY

From a grove of trees on a dark, starry night rise multiple rickety ladders with worn-out rungs, reaching for the heavens. But they can't get very far, can't bridge the expansive gap. Graciously, another ladder, bright and sturdy, descends from above. In this still frame it's just peeping its legs in, but presumably its downward movement will continue until it touches all the way down to earth.

This woodcut captures a sense of human yearning for God—our desire to access and connect with transcendent reality—and God's merciful condescension that makes such connection possible. In the Incarnation God put on flesh and lowered himself down to us, embodying divine love in our midst and creating a concourse between heaven and earth. He made a way, a high way, in our wilderness, where there was no way. The cross-shaped stars that glint in the background allude to Jesus's cruciform ministry that culminated in his atoning death.

Steps and ladders are a common motif in the work of Donald Furst (born 1953), an artist of faith who uses a variety of printmaking media, including engraving, etching, linoleum cut, lithography, mezzotint, screen printing, solarplate intaglio, vitreography, and woodcut. Furst retired this May from the faculty of the University of North Carolina at Wilmington's Department of Art and Art History, where he taught since 1985.

HIGH WAY
Donald Furst, 2010
Woodcut, 13 × 8 in.
www.donaldfurst.com

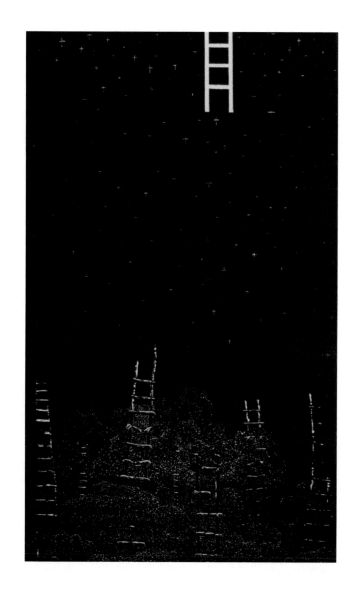

The Visitation

BY GLORIA GUEVARA

"I'm bursting with God-news;
I'm dancing the song of my Savior God.
God took one good look at me,
and look what happened—
I'm the most fortunate woman on earth!

What God has done for me will never be forgotten,
the God whose very name is holy, set apart from all others.
His mercy flows in wave after wave
on those who are in awe before him.
He bared his arm and showed his strength,
scattered the bluffing braggarts.
He knocked tyrants off their high horses,
pulled victims out of the mud.
The starving poor sat down to a banquet;
the callous rich were left out in the cold . . ."

—Luke 1:46–53 (MSG)

CURATOR COMMENTARY

Voiced by Mary in Luke 1:46–55 during her visit to her cousin Elizabeth's house, the Magnificat is one of the oldest and most radical Advent hymns. It speaks of the coming reign of God and the power inversion brought along with it—of collapsing thrones and the elevation of the poor, of the hungry being filled and the rich sent away empty. Mary sings a song of revolution, of justice and liberation, one that has carried special resonance for oppressed communities around the world.

Painted just four years after the overthrow of the dictatorial Somoza regime in Nicaragua, *The Visitation* by Gloria Guevara (born 1954) sets Mary's recitation of the Magnificat in her own island home of Solentiname, whose lush vegetation and surrounding blue lake waters are visible through the open window in the back. A Hispanic Mary, pregnant with the Good News, lifts her hands in prophetic proclamation before her elder relative. Even Elizabeth's dog wags its tail in excitement at her words! The fruit on the nearby table echoes the fruitfulness of Mary's own rounded body, bearing Jesus Christ, and that of Elizabeth, bearing John the Forerunner, an Advent figure.

Guevara is part of a Christian community and school of painters founded in Solentiname in 1966 by the Nicaraguan priest, poet, and political revolutionary Ernesto Cardenal (1925–2020). They find hope and empowerment in the gospel of Jesus, not just for the next life but for this one as well.

THE VISITATION

Gloria Guevara, 1981

Source: *The Gospel in Art by the Peasants of Solentiname*, ed. Philip and Sally Scharper

Prayers, Part 2

THURSDAY MORNING *to* SATURDAY EVENING

GERMANY

Thomas Bormans

Thursday Morning

MORNING PRAYER

CALL

Give ear to my words, O LORD; consider my groaning.
Give attention to the sound of my cry,
my King and my God, for to you do I pray.
Psalm 5:1-2

PSALM

Read the Psalm of the day.

THE O ANTIPHONS

O Adonai,
and leader of the house of Israel,
who appeared to Moses in the fire of the burning bush
and gave him the law on Sinai:
come and redeem us with an outstretched arm.

Taken from *The New Ancient Collects*

ADORATION

SILENCE OR SONG

Seasonal song selections can be found on pp. 57-63.

LESSON

Read the New Testament passage of the day.

PRAYER

Grant us, O God, a vision of our land
that is as beautiful as it could be:
a land of justice where none shall prey on others;
a land of plenty where poverty shall cease to fester;
a land of kinship where success
shall be founded on service;
a land of peace where order shall rest not on force
but on the love of everyone for their community.
Give us grace to put this vision into practice
through Jesus Christ our Lord.

Adapted from a prayer of the Christian Council of Nigeria

ABIDING

LECTIO DIVINA, VISIO DIVINA, OR PRAXIO DIVINA

Pause at the start of a new day. Enjoy communion with the living God:
Father, Son, and Holy Spirit. Listen for the voice of God in the scriptures.
Read. Meditate. Pray. Contemplate. Seek God's face.

PROMPTED PRAYER

- For individuals and faith communities recovering from scandal or spiritual abuse
- For people who are experiencing homelessness or instability with their housing
- For those who are struggling to believe in God's goodness

THE LORD'S PRAYER

Our Father who art in heaven, hallowed be thy name.
Thy kingdom come, thy will be done,
on earth as it is in heaven.
Give us this day our daily bread;
and forgive us our debts, as we forgive our debtors.
And lead us not into temptation, but deliver us from evil.
For thine is the kingdom and the power
and the glory, forever. Amen.

BENEDICTION

"Sing and rejoice, O daughter of Zion, for behold, I
come and I will dwell in your midst," declares the
LORD. "And many nations shall join themselves
to the LORD in that day, and shall be my people.
And I will dwell in your midst." May you commune
with the indwelling Spirit throughout this day.

Adapted from Zechariah 2:10–11a

LECTIONARY

DEC 19

THE PURIFIER

Ps. 16

Mal. 4:1–6

Luke 1:1–25

MORNING PRAYER

Thursday Evening

LECTIONARY

DEC 5

THE PEACE

Ps. 4

Gen. 4:1–16

Heb. 12:22–29

DEC 12

THE TABERNACLE

Ps. 10

Exod. 40:33–38

Rev. 21:22–22:5

CALL

O LORD, God of my salvation,
I cry out day and night before you.

Psalm 88:1

PSALM

Read the Psalm of the day.

THE O ANTIPHONS

O Adonai,
and leader of the house of Israel,
who appeared to Moses in the fire of the burning bush
and gave him the law on Sinai:
come and redeem us with an outstretched arm.

Taken from *The New Ancient Collects*

ADORATION

SILENCE OR SONG

Seasonal song selections can be found on pp. 57-63.

LESSON

Read the Old Testament passage of the day.

PRAYER

Father, Son, and Holy Spirit,
to all nations grant unity, peace, and concord,
and to all people give dignity, food, and shelter.
Hear us, good Lord.
Grant us abundant harvests, strength
and skill to conserve the resources of the
earth, and wisdom to use them well.
Hear us, good Lord.
Come to the help of all who are in danger, necessity,
and trouble; protect all who travel by land, air, or water;
and show your pity on all prisoners and captives.
Hear us, good Lord.
Strengthen and preserve all women who are in
childbirth, and all young children, and comfort
the aged, the bereaved, and the lonely.
Hear us, good Lord.

Defend and provide for the widowed and the orphaned, the refugees and the homeless, the unemployed, and all who are desolate and oppressed.
Hear us, good Lord.
Heal those who are sick in body or mind, and give skill and compassion to all who care for them.
Hear us, good Lord.
Grant us true repentance, forgive our sins, and strengthen us by your Holy Spirit to amend our lives according to your Holy Word.
Hear us, good Lord. Amen.

A form of the Great Litany adapted from *The Book of Common Worship.* The Great Litany is derived from ancient forms of Christian prayer that date back to the liturgy of John Chrysostom in the fourth century.

ABIDING

LECTIO DIVINA, VISIO DIVINA, OR PRAXIO DIVINA

Pause at the start of a new day. Enjoy communion with the living God: Father, Son, and Holy Spirit. Listen for the voice of God in the scriptures. Read. Meditate. Pray. Contemplate. Seek God's face.

INTERCESSORY PRAYER

Pray for the known needs of your church, neighborhood, city, and world.

BENEDICTION

"He will wipe away every tear from their eyes, and death shall be no more, neither shall there be mourning, nor crying, nor pain anymore, for the former things have passed away." And he who was seated on the throne said, "Behold, I am making all things new." Also he said, "Write this down, for these words are trustworthy and true." May you rest now in this promise of restoration.

Adapted from Revelation 21:4–5

LECTIONARY

DEC 19

THE PURIFIER

Ps. 16

Mal. 4:1–6

Luke 1:1–25

EVENING PRAYER

Friday Morning

MORNING PRAYER

CALL

With joy you will draw water
from the wells of salvation.
And you will say in that day:
"Give thanks to the LORD, call upon his name."

Isaiah 12:3–4

PSALM

Read the Psalm of the day.

THE O ANTIPHONS

O King of the nations,
and their desire,
the cornerstone making both one:
come and save the human race,
which you fashioned from clay.

Taken from *The New Ancient Collects*

ADORATION

SILENCE OR SONG

Seasonal song selections can be found on pp. 57–63.

LESSON

Read the Old Testament passage of the day.

PRAYER

O Lord, we come this morning
Knee-bowed and body-bent
Before Thy throne of grace.
O Lord—this morning—
Bow our hearts beneath our knees,
And our knees in some lonesome valley.
We come this morning—
Like empty pitchers to a full fountain,
With no merits of our own.

O Lord—open up a window of heaven,
And lean out far over the battlements of glory,
And listen this morning.

A prayer of James Weldon Johnson (1871–1938), taken from *God's Trombones*. Johnson was an author, politician, diplomat, literary critic, journalist, poet, anthologist, educator, lawyer, songwriter, and early civil rights activist.

ABIDING

LECTIO DIVINA, VISIO DIVINA, OR PRAXIO DIVINA

Pause at the start of a new day. Enjoy communion with the living God: Father, Son, and Holy Spirit. Listen for the voice of God in the scriptures. Read. Meditate. Pray. Contemplate. Seek God's face.

PROMPTED PRAYER

- For curiosity and openness toward your neighbors
- For the ability to offer care to someone who is suffering
- For public libraries and those who work in them

THE LORD'S PRAYER

Our Father who art in heaven, hallowed be thy name.
Thy kingdom come, thy will be done,
on earth as it is in heaven.
Give us this day our daily bread;
and forgive us our debts, as we forgive our debtors.
And lead us not into temptation, but deliver us from evil.
For thine is the kingdom and the power
and the glory, forever. Amen.

BENEDICTION

May grace be with you.

Adapted from 1 Timothy 6:21

LECTIONARY

DEC 20

THE PROMISED

OFFSPRING

Ps. 17

2 Kings 17:18–23;
25:8–11

Matt. 1:1–23

MORNING PRAYER

Friday Evening

LECTIONARY

DEC 6

THE FLOOD

Ps. 5

Gen. 7:1–10, 17–24

Luke 17:22–37

DEC 13

THE PRIEST

Ps. 11

Exod. 28:1–5

Heb. 9:11–14

CALL

Yet God my King is from of old,
working salvation in the midst of the earth.
Yours is the day, yours also the night.

Psalm 74:12, 16a

PSALM

Read the Psalm of the day.

THE O ANTIPHONS

O King of the nations,
and their desire,
the cornerstone making both one:
come and save the human race,
which you fashioned from clay.

Taken from *The New Ancient Collects*

ADORATION

SILENCE OR SONG

Seasonal song selections can be found on pp. 57-63.

LESSON

Read the New Testament passage of the day.

PRAYER

Kindle the flint, the tinder
Liven the hearth, the stone
Shelter the dying lantern light
Gladden the shadowed home
Into this wilderness of shadows
Come, Light original

Answer our famine yearning
Nourish our blighted fields
Raise all our fallen storehouses
Leaven the bitter yield
Into this emptiness, this hunger
Come, Bread all-bountiful

Loosen the cloaks of journeymen
Mend all the broken roads
Wake us from fitful forest sleep
Lighten the lonely load
Into this pilgrimage, this journey
Come, Home perpetual

Come, Light
Come, Bread
Come, Home
Come

A prayer adapted from the song "Come Light" by Gregory Thompson

ABIDING

LECTIO DIVINA, VISIO DIVINA, OR PRAXIO DIVINA

Pause at the start of a new day. Enjoy communion with the living God: Father, Son, and Holy Spirit. Listen for the voice of God in the scriptures. Read. Meditate. Pray. Contemplate. Seek God's face.

INTERCESSORY PRAYER

Pray for the known needs of your church, neighborhood, city, and world.

BENEDICTION

Now may our Lord Jesus Christ himself, and God our Father, who loved us and gave us eternal comfort and good hope through grace, comfort your hearts and establish them in every good work and word.

2 Thessalonians 2:16–17

LECTIONARY

DEC 20

THE PROMISED

OFFSPRING

Ps. 17

2 Kings 17:18–23;

25:8–11

Matt. 1:1–23

EVENING PRAYER

Saturday Morning

MORNING PRAYER

CALL
Our soul waits for the LORD;
he is our help and our shield.
Psalm 33:20

PSALM
Read the Psalm of the day.

THE O ANTIPHONS
O Root of Jesse,
standing as a sign among the peoples,
before you kings will shut their mouths;
to you the nations will make their prayer.
Come and deliver us, and delay no longer.
Taken from *The New Ancient Collects*

ADORATION
SILENCE OR SONG
Seasonal song selections can be found on pp. 57–63.

LESSON
Read the New Testament passage of the day.

CREED
We believe in one God, the Father Almighty, who made the heaven and the earth and the seas and all the things that are in them. We believe in Christ Jesus, the Son of God, who was made flesh for our salvation. We believe in the Holy Spirit, who made known through the prophets the plan of salvation, and Christ's coming, and the birth from a virgin, and the passion, and the resurrection from the dead, and the bodily ascension into heaven of the beloved Christ Jesus. Jesus is our Lord, and in the future he will appear from heaven in the glory of the Father to sum up all things and to raise anew all flesh of the whole human race.
The "Rule of Faith" by Irenaeus (125–202 CE) of Smyrna (present-day Izmir, Turkey), adapted from his work *Adversus haereses*

PRAYER

Sunrise marks the hour for us to begin our toil,
but in our souls, Lord, prepare a dwelling for the
day that will never end. Grant that we may come to
know the risen life and that nothing may distract
us from the delights you offer. Through our
unremitting zeal for you, Lord, set upon us the
sign of your day that is not measured by the sun.

A prayer of Ephrem the Syrian (ca. 306–373 CE)

ABIDING

LECTIO DIVINA, VISIO DIVINA, OR PRAXIO DIVINA

Pause at the start of a new day. Enjoy communion with the living God:
Father, Son, and Holy Spirit. Listen for the voice of God in the scriptures.
Read. Meditate. Pray. Contemplate. Seek God's face.

PROMPTED PRAYER

- For humility and adaptability to life's interruptions
- For a heart that longs and watches for the coming of the Lord
- For a taste of God's rest this Sabbath

THE LORD'S PRAYER

Our Father who art in heaven, hallowed be thy name.
Thy kingdom come, thy will be done,
on earth as it is in heaven.
Give us this day our daily bread;
and forgive us our debts, as we forgive our debtors.
And lead us not into temptation, but deliver us from evil.
For thine is the kingdom and the power
and the glory, forever. Amen.

BENEDICTION

For behold, darkness shall cover the earth, and
thick darkness the peoples; but the LORD will arise
upon you, and his glory will be seen upon you.
And nations shall come to your light, and kings
to the brightness of your rising. May you walk
forward in grace as you follow the Risen One.

Adapted from Isaiah 60:2–3

LECTIONARY

DEC 21

THE HEALER

Ps. 18

Jer. 8:18–9:1

Matt. 8:5–17

MORNING PRAYER

Saturday Morning

LECTIONARY

DEC 7

THE SON OF ABRAHAM

Ps. 6

Gen. 11:27–12:9

Gal. 3:8–14

DEC 14

THE SACRIFICE

Ps. 12

Lev. 16:29–34

Heb. 9:23–28

CALL

Let my prayer be counted as incense before you,
and the lifting up of my hands as the evening sacrifice!
Psalm 141:2

PSALM

Read the Psalm of the day.

THE O ANTIPHONS

O Root of Jesse,
standing as a sign among the peoples,
before you kings will shut their mouths;
to you the nations will make their prayer.
Come and deliver us, and delay no longer.

Taken from *The New Ancient Collects*

ADORATION

SILENCE OR SONG

Seasonal song selections can be found on pp. 57–63.

LESSON

Read the Old Testament passage of the day.

PRAYER

CONFESSION: Lamb of God, you take away
the sins of the world, have mercy on us.
Lamb of God, you take away the sins
of the world, have mercy on us.
Lamb of God, you take away the sins
of the world, grant us peace.

The Agnus Dei

ASSURANCE: Christ, our Passover lamb, has been
sacrificed. Let us therefore celebrate the festival, not
with the old leaven, the leaven of malice and evil, but
with the unleavened bread of sincerity and truth.

1 Corinthians 5:7–8

ABIDING

LECTIO DIVINA, VISIO DIVINA, OR PRAXIO DIVINA

Pause at the start of a new day. Enjoy communion with the living God: Father, Son, and Holy Spirit. Listen for the voice of God in the scriptures. Read. Meditate. Pray. Contemplate. Seek God's face.

PRAYER OF MINDFULNESS

1. Become aware of God's presence.
2. Review this past week with gratitude.
3. Pay attention to your emotions.
4. Choose one feature of the week and pray from it.
5. Look toward tomorrow and the beginning of a new week.

A PRAYER FOR SABBATH

Creator God,
on the seventh day you rested and were refreshed.
Please help me now to enter into
the rest of your Sabbath,
that I may cease from my work
and delight in your care over my life
both now and forever.
Amen.

BENEDICTION

Lord, you now have set your servants free to go in peace as you have promised, for these eyes of ours have seen the savior, whom you have prepared for all the world to see: a light to enlighten the nations, and the glory of your people Israel. Glory to the Father, and to the Son, and to the Holy Spirit: as it was in the beginning, is now, and will be forever. Amen.

The Nunc Dimittis (Song of Simeon), based on Luke 2:29-32

LECTIONARY

DEC 21

THE HEALER

Ps. 18

Jer. 8:18–9:1

Matt. 8:5–17

EVENING PRAYER

Songbook

for ADORATION

CHINA

Xingchen Yan

Come, Thou Long-Expected Jesus

Come, thou long—— ex - pec - ted Je - sus,
Born thy peo - ple to de - li - ver,

born to set thy peo - ple free;
born a child and yet—— a King,

from our fears—— and sins re - lease—— us,
born to reign—— in us for - ev - er,

let us find our rest—— in thee.
now thy gra - cious king - dom bring.

Is - rael's strength and con - so - la - tion,
By thine own—— e - ter - nal spi - rit

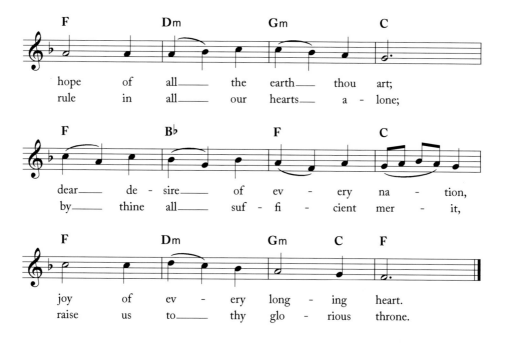

hope of all___ the earth___ thou art;
rule in all___ our hearts___ a - lone;

dear___ de - sire___ of ev - ery na - tion,
by___ thine all___ suf - fi - cient mer - it,

joy of ev - ery long - ing heart.
raise us to___ thy glo - rious throne.

Words by Charles Wesley (1707–1788) of England. Music by Rowland Prichard (1811–1887) of Wales.

Tenemos Esperanza
(We Have Hope)

Words by Federico J. Pagura (1923–2016) of Argentina. Music by Homero R. Perera of Argentina,

TRANSLATION

VERSE 1: Because he came into the world and history
Because he broke the silence and the agony
Because he filled the earth with his glory
Because he was light in our cold night
Because he was born in a dark manger
Because he lived sowing love and life
Because he opened up the hard hearts
And lifted up the downcast souls

CHORUS: That's why we have hope today
That's why we fight tenaciously today
That's why today we look with confidence
To the future of this land of mine
That's why we have hope today
That's why we fight tenaciously today
That's why today we look with confidence
To the future

VERSE 2: Because he attacked the ambitious merchants
And denounced evil and hypocrisy
Because he exalted the children, the women
And rejected those who burned with pride
Because he carried the cross of our suffering
And tasted the bitterness of our ills
Because he accepted to suffer our condemnation
And thus died for all mortals

VERSE 3: Because a dawn saw his great victory
Over death, the fear, the lies
Now nothing can stop his story
Or the coming of his eternal kingdom
Because he brightens every path with glory
And he defeated darkness with light
Because his light is always our story
And ought to take everyone to the mountaintop

Wait for the Lord

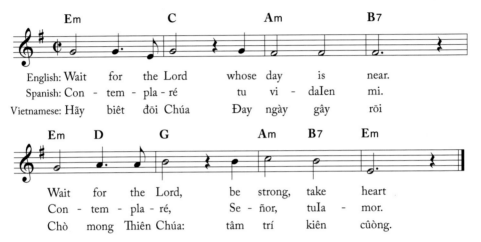

English: Wait for the Lord whose day is near.
Spanish: Con - tem - pla - ré tu vi - daIen mi.
Vietnamese: Hãy biêt đõi Chúa Đay ngày gây rõi

Wait for the Lord, be strong, take heart
Con - tem - pla - ré, Se - ñor, tuIa - mor.
Chò mong Thiên Chúa: tâm trí kiên cûòng.

Words: The Taizé Community. Music: Jacques Berthier (1923–1994). © 1984 Les Presses de Taizé,

GIA Publications, Inc., agent. All rights reserved. Used with permission.

Come Light Our Hearts

Words and music by Sandra McCracken. © 2014 Drink Your Tea (ASCAP), admin. by Music Services.

Made in the USA
Monee, IL
14 November 2024

69832277R00038